I Suck at Pronouns

Confessions of the Mom of a Transgender Boy

RENEE MASTERSON-CARR

PAGE PUBLISHING, INC.
Conneaut Lake, PA

First originally published by Page Publishing 2020

ISBN 978-1-6624-1393-3 (pbk)
ISBN 978-1-6624-1394-0 (digital)

Printed in the United States of America

Contents

Chapter 1

In the Beginning

Okay, I'll admit it, I did always want a boy. I was always a tomboy myself and honestly wouldn't have known exactly what to do with a girly girl. However, you just want a healthy baby! Boy or girl, it doesn't matter, as long as it's healthy.

So at thirty-three, I was told that I was having a girl. And to make a long story short, after the doctors told me that she most likely had downs syndrome and would probably be a dwarf, I panicked a bit. Okay, I panicked a lot, and I cried a lot. But after the third month, they simply said, "Oh no, she's fine. We had the wrong date. My bad." (Insert eye roll here.)

Six months later, I had a perfect baby with nines across the board—a perfectly developing baby that grew into a perfectly destructive toddler. I slept very little, as did the child. I probably had a bit of postpartum depression, but I figure the sleep-deprived often do. I very often didn't want to leave this little munchkin so that I could take care of myself, and that may have been wrong, but who knows. I only wanted to leave her with her father, and he was busy starting up his own company and had very little time for anything other than that. No, I'm not blaming him. I'm just trying to show you my mindset at the time. I'd love to say that there is no book on parenting, but let's face it, there are hundreds. Of course, they all contradict each other, so you're back to square one.

Just a little more background here—after her second birthday, her father and I started to have marital issues. There might have been signs previous to that, but I was busy with a little one and never saw them. It ended in divorce. Of course, it was hard at first, but we never let her see any arguing. She was nary aware that there were any issues at all, Luckily, he was and is a very busy executive, so his change of residence barely went noticed at that young age. Soon enough, he had remarried, and our little one then had three loving parents. Not long after, I fell in love, and she then had four loving parents. And yes, the boy still does have four loving parents.

Chapter 2

Don't Judge

Now before you judge me as one of those moms who pushed their child to be a certain gender, I am not. She wore pink and tutus, had eight million stuffed animals, played dress-up, and played with Barbie just as much as playing in sports and with dinosaurs, Star Wars, as well as the many trips to the space museum. I never played a gender card simply because I never had the gender card placed on me.

As a child, I wore pretty dresses. I made mud pies, played sports, played with Barbie, crashed my bicycle, and swam circles around the boys. I like to think I'm perfectly normal, but...well, you know, what exactly is *normal*? I'm a female carpenter. I played football and boxed. I'm the size of an average NFL running back, but damn if I can't rock an evening gown and a pair of stilettos! I will also admit that I had conversations with friends, at which time I stated that I would be perfectly okay if she turned out to be a lesbian because then I wouldn't have to worry about teen pregnancy (yeah, well, I am a *Gilmore Girl* fan after all). This was half joking and half "eh, not a bad idea." And yes, being a lesbian isn't exactly an easy life either, even in the early twenty-first century, but I certainly didn't have a problem with it, should that be her lifestyle. In lieu of all that, I just never saw any of the "transgender signs" that the professionals speak of. Nothing seemed "out of the ordinary," and I don't think any teachers picked up on it until junior high school.

During the early years, when the girl bullies started (which they always do at some point), you know, the "frenemies," the "mean girls," I told her that she'd be better off figuring out which of the boys in the class was the gay boy and latch onto him (there's always at least one). Gay boys make the best girlfriends! Any woman who has a gay male friend knows I speak the truth! They will tell you the truth when you look like crap. They have no problem holding your purse when you try on clothes, play with your hair, and they know exactly which cute boy is the one to go for and which is not. Now when I said this to her, I had absolutely no idea that she would take heed in these words, and not only she befriended them but also became one.

She was a bit of a late bloomer (which is perfectly fine with just about *any* mom), so when puberty hit, mid-junior high, that's when we started to notice something a little different. She tried the girly things, dresses for special events, even tried a little makeup, but it all seemed forced. Maybe she still wasn't sure who she was, and I certainly wasn't making that decision.

Here's the interesting part. At that point, she went from a little dress-up girl to an uber girl. She went full force into the cutesy dresses, long gorgeous locks of hair, makeup, painted nails, and high heels. I was like, "Okay, this is it. This is where my little girl becomes a woman." I had no idea what was going on inside her. I did, however, find out from the therapist later on that this is somewhat standard for transgender people. As they don't know what's going on inside, they try to gracefully nudge what they believe is natural. The confusion she initially felt inside was only amplified by the over-the-top cover-up and added greatly to her anxiety and depression.

Not long after that, she wanted to cut off her beautiful hair and shop in the boys' clothes department. She took out her earrings—all the usual prompts to look more boyish. I started thinking, maybe she was a lesbian because whatever was going on was a little more than your average tomboy. I am and was completely okay with this idea. Never in a million years did I think, "Oh yeah, my kid is transgender." It just didn't come to mind, or at least it didn't.

I realized pretty early on that she was at least bi-sexual. Again, no big deal, pretty normal as far as the twenty-first century goes and the late twentieth, I think. I remember having an easy conversation one day in the car when I pretty much blurted out that I know that she's part of the LGBTQ community. The kid was pretty shocked that I saw it, although I'm not sure exactly why. I guess all teens think their parents are completely unaware. LOL.

About this time, our very outgoing little girl became a lot more reserved, just wanting to stay in her room. She had a select few friends, who were also in the LGBTQ community. She was a little overweight and started getting very depressed and anxious about dealing with the extended family on holidays. (I only mentioned the weight because we thought maybe that had something to do with the teen depression.) She started getting very dark. Her normally beautiful art drawings started to have dire connotations. She tried to get out of going to her father's house on his weekends because he lived on the other end of New Jersey, and she was away from the friends that made her feel normal. Her father saw this first, and we decided to bring her to see someone.

We found an amazing therapist whom he loves! We started at twice per week and now are down to twice per month. He was diagnosed with dysphoria. With that disorder, social anxiety and depression usually come hand in hand, and they did. He was diagnosed with all three. The diagnosis made dealing with this change a little easier, a little.

I love my kid unconditionally and will do anything for him! But if anyone thinks that dealing with dysphoria is simple, they are utterly mistaken…as the person with it or the parents thereof. It's a whole other life skill to comprehend and learn, and they certainly don't teach that in school. And we researched and learned as much as we could!

You may have noticed that my writings switched pronouns. Well, this is about when *his* pronoun changed.

Chapter 3

Dysphoria and Trans-Trenders

There's a public outcry that being transgender is a mental disorder. Well, technically, it is, at least. It's the result of dysphoria, which is a mental disorder. As per Wikipedia, *gender dysphoria is discomfort, unhappiness, or distress due to one's gender or physical sex. The current edition (DSM-5) of the Diagnostic and Statistical Manual of Mental Disorders uses the term "gender dysphoria" where it previously referred to "gender identity disorder," making it clear that they no longer consider the gender identity to be disordered but rather the emotional state of distress which results from the gender identity.*

That's a basic definition, at least, and you'll probably have to read it four or five times to even grasp an iota of it (yes, me too). With dysphoria, a person does not like what they see in the mirror. It's like they're looking at a reflection that doesn't agree with what they see and feel inside their own mind as if they're looking at someone else. They'll do anything not to look in a mirror and to avoid anything that remotely resembles the gender they were born into. For example, my kid would cover the mirrors in the bathroom when he needed to get naked to shower. He'd put a towel over his lap while using the toilet. He'd take selfies but only above the chest. He binds his chest and wears turtlenecks to cover his lack of Adam's apple. He slouched a lot and avoided public areas, especially when a binder is inconvenient (such as working out or beach activities). However, we did finally find a binder company that has a swim binder. It was not as tight and could wear under a rash guard. He didn't want to work out because he couldn't wear his binder, as it's dangerous to bind and exercise, and then you'd also see his chest—and so would he.

He's been in therapy now for a few years. It is very important to find a therapist who is informed of dysphoria! I can't state this enough. Therapy is not going to be a quick "fix" to his mental state. He's also in group therapy with some other LGBTQ teens that has helped tremendously. He was diagnosed with dysphoria, social anxiety and depression, which I mentioned. And the group has helped tremendously as well as herbal supplements. We agreed not to put him on medications as no one wants to lose this wonderful child. St. John's Wort helps him, but I in no way endorse it or anything other than your own research. That's between the individual and their doctor!

So all in all, I'd have to say that yes, being transgender can most likely be associated with a mental disorder. But so are a million other socially accepted ways of life. Call it what you will, but it's real. It's here, and it's not going away anytime soon.

There are the select few transgender individuals that say they do not have dysphoria. But after conversations with quite a few transgender people at a conference, they all agreed that there's something inaccurate about that view. It does, however, lead to the conclusion that there may be another mental disorder involved or maybe just some very confused or curious people, but that's for another story.

I love my kid and will do anything for him! But dysphoria is not easy or fake, and dealing with this is a daunting, long process. As the person with it or the parents thereof, it's a whole other life skill to learn, and we did because I love my kid and will do anything for him!

It's not to say that there aren't fakes out there or what my kid calls "trans-trenders." These are the people that make our lives a living hell. They seek attention. They criminalize activities. They give the true transgender community a harsh stigma that the public uses to defend the anti-transgender movement. They make it difficult to get gender-neutral bathrooms or for a true transgender person to use the only facility they are comfortable in because people are afraid of the fakes, the molesters misusing the public trust. And in all fairness, the fear is understood. But as I said, it just makes our lives more difficult. As the mother of a transgender boy, I am afraid every time I send him into a public men's room—not for fear of the fakes, but for fear of the ignorant. His father and I have had many conversations regarding this, and both of us have an eye twitch, but...

We've recently released the reigns a little, and I cringe, but it's necessary. A little piece of my heart breaks every time, hoping that he won't get bullied, beat up, or, God forbid, raped. I've watched *Boys Don't Cry* endless times, and it is by far my greatest fear. The only saving grace is knowing that Brandon Teena had very little support at home and ran, whereas we couldn't support our young man more. We worry a little less at a local restaurant or store, and I will search for the family restroom at a larger venue, such as an arena. They're usually available but hard to find. If you find a security guard, they'll usually lead you in the right direction without too much questioning. We've been directed to an employee-only lounge more than once by a considerate security guard (usually female, I have to say).

Every mother worries when they start sending their teen out into the world on their own—some more than others. I'm one of the "more," not because my baby is growing up, but more because he's been bullied since he was ten, and those bullies are growing up too. Yes, some having woken up to our new world. But there are still so many ignorant people out there with a willingness to torture anything they don't understand. So yes, I probably worry more than the average bear mom, or maybe that's just what makes me a bear mom. But I suck it up. I try my best, and I give the stink eye to the bullies when I see them.

As I stated before, a therapist has helped him tremendously—so has meditation! I recommend teaching the kid how to meditate—take them to a studio class. It will help a great deal!

In addition to what I just consider a direct path of therapy and meditation, once an individual wants to start transitioning, a good doctor would want to have the individual evaluated to determine the need for these hormones and surgeries, so therapy may actually be a necessity. If you've already started it, then you're a step ahead. If your insurance pays for gender reassignment, the evaluation will definitely be required for them. I know that we personally need an evaluation from the therapist with his diagnosis so that the school can institute the name/gender changes.

You may have noticed that my writings switched to male pronouns. Well, that's because his pronoun changed.

Chapter 4

Names and Pronouns

I gave birth to a beautiful baby girl—perfect in every way, except… except there was something in my baby girl that was going to pop out its gorgeous head sooner or later. So now I have a handsome young man.

Around eleven or twelve, I noticed him squirm every time someone would call him by his birth name. So I started using gender-neutral terms when talking to or about him. He was the "kiddo," my "shmoo," the "child," etc. I never used his given name on social media, and I went from using the pronoun "she" to "the kid did this" or "that child of mine blah blah blah." I changed his name in my cell to "o spawn of my loins." It made him happier. He stood a little taller, but it still wasn't right.

One day, I caught a friend of his calling him by a male name. I'm sure I raised one eyebrow (insert Mr. Spock's impression here) in question because he saw it. So once we were alone, conversation #2. I believe the conversation started with "Sooooooooo—" I didn't have to finish the question because he knew exactly where I was headed.

"Yeah, my friends call me Keith."

"Okay, so is that the name you're going to be for the rest of your life?" He shrugged. I sighed.

I have to say that at this point in his life, I realized that a good 95 percent of the friends/kids coming over and hanging out were in the LGBTQ community, which is more than acceptable with me!!

The only problem I had was that they *all* kept changing names and genders—boy, then girl, then gender-neutral, then cosmic (or comic-a seemingly endless array of X-men), then back to girl, boy, etc. This is beyond confusing for a fifty-year-old mom. The pronouns kept changing as well—she, he, they, back to she. It got harder and harder to keep track of who was who. I tried to keep up (I still do), but it's extremely difficult, especially since I was brought up with the knowledge that "they" referred to a group of people, not an individual who is gender-neutral. Again, I'm trying, but guess what, I suck at pronouns! I mean, I really do. At a conference, we were to write our pronoun on our name tag. What did this idiot do? I wrote Mom. Seriously, could I have been more of a moron? It was not even a pronoun. SMDH. At some point, I plundered a fresh name tag from an unmanned table and retracted my original pronoun, unbeknownst to the powers that be.

It also happens that a few of these cosmic kids appear to be the "trenders," and I don't foresee them continuing on the transgender path past college, but hey, you never know. Some are also bullies who happen to try to make minions of the anxiety-ridden, shy, depressed LGBTQ kids, and it does work. The "outcasts" feel welcomed by these strong personalities and scoop in right under their proverbial wings and take on their X-men roles that their adolescent professor gives them. The problem then lies with the age. These are preteens and teens looking for a place to fit in. And they do. They find their niche. This alpha gives them a new name, and they go about their happy lives until…until they grow up a little. They no longer see life through their alpha's angry eyes. They know they're loved. They find a new place and don't agree with alpha's theories. It's just high school BS but with a twist, a very, very confused, difficult twist. And the name changes again.

What I did learn immediately was that "it" is probably the *worst* term I could possibly have ever used! I didn't mean it in a derogatory way. I just didn't know what to say half the time. Luckily, my kid understood my frustration and didn't get angry, just corrected me each time—sometimes with side-eye. Over time, it's gotten a bit easier, but *that* one I figured out how *not* to use.

Now my parents are another story. They're in their seventies. We've explained the situation, had talks, given them pamphlets to read, websites to go to, but I think you know where this is going. They love this kid unconditionally and are trying so, so hard, but did I mention that they're in their seventies? My dad is the true Archie Bunker stereotype, ex-Marine (always a Marine), and I definitely give him more credit than most! He's actually calling him by his new name, which I have to admit shocked the crap out of me! My mom's a lot more liberal, and using the new name came easier for her. But I am constantly correcting them in the pronoun area.

Mind you, everyone still screws up on occasion (including me). It's only been a few years, and he still hasn't started hormone transitioning (more on that later), which I believe will make the pronoun game a lot easier. I constantly have to correct the grandparental units though. I've explained to the kid that this older generation is going to be a lot tougher than mine and mine a bit tougher than millennials and so on. But I thank everything holy that the kid completely understands this concept. He doesn't like it, but he understands it! My mother, on the other hand, gets annoyed when I correct her. If I hear "get over it" one more time, I may completely lose my shit. However, I have explained to her that she needs to do this for him. If he's kind enough not to get upset with her for forgetting, then she needs to "get over it" when we correct her. This is an ongoing process. Again, sigh.

They're not the only ones either. It seems that once you're completely set in your ways (sometime over the age of fifty), any change is arduous. And this type of change is a biggie! I'm not sure if they'll ever get it. I have quite a few older friends and religious friends that I know will never quite grasp the concept. It doesn't necessarily make them bad people. It's just hard to teach an old dog new tricks.

Screwing up or forgetting is one thing. Not understanding what you're seeing or reading is another. Now mind you, I'm part of a mom group of which some don't even know when they're supposed to cross the street. So I really don't expect much from the general population.

But I've watched the news and social media and heard all these people completely losing their composure when it comes to pronouns and refusing to use the one that makes the individual happy. I don't get that. Honestly, what difference does it make? If she wants to be called "he," just do it. It's not hurting you or anyone else. It's just a word, just a pronoun. And it sure as hell makes that individual just a little happier. Don't we all just like to be a little happier?

Chapter 5

A Little Background

So this kid of mine is a very awesome human being. He's smart, really smart, maybe too smart for his own good (and I might add, he does occasionally come across as a little arrogant—but hey, so do his parents every so often). He was accepted to the most accredited public high school in our county for their engineering program (which he then decided he wasn't interested in—se la vi). He holds a 4.5 GPA, takes a few AP courses, and every teacher loves him.

As a matter of fact, every adult loves him. Teachers that strike fear in many of the students buy *him* end-of-year presents. He's kind, loving, respectful, caring, well-spoken, and an extremely talented artist, hence no longer having an interest in engineering. He's in the drama club (well duh), the chess club, and the LGBT club (again, duh). He holds a position in the stigma-free club and the animation club and is the exchange student ambassador because he can speak the basics in four languages and is extremely personable. He's also a peer leader. (I think I just wrote his resume accidentally.)

Okay, so yes, I'm biased. But I bet you couldn't go into his school and find an adult to discredit me! Now people don't have the same opinion of me, but something happened on the way to fifty. I just don't care what people think of me. I'm here to make sure my kid has a good life and is a happy, healthy, and contributing member of society. I'm not Mother Theresa, so it's perfectly fine if you don't like me. I've made some enemies on the way, trying to open a few doors for the transgender community in our little community, and again, I don't care. I know there are people who avoid me like the plague. I have a very outspoken personality, and maybe this is why I'm made the way I am—to help and protect a couple of kids who are having some trouble getting their voices heard.

Reminder: Early on, we weren't sure what was going on, as I said. So we kind of took it all in with a grain of salt. When this all begins, you don't know if your kid is a true transgender individual or if they're just being trendy or trying to fit into a group that accepts just about anyone because they're kind of a misfit. Back in the eighties, I was a misfit too, albeit not gay, but our group of misfits consisted of the head-banging metalheads that accepted anyone as our own. Of course, it's very different today, and that's why I am so forthcoming about therapy. You do need to make sure this is a definite mental state before choosing to do any nonreversible physical changes!

Chapter 6

Pick a Name

So it started with the Keith reference from one of his peers. I could tell he wasn't exactly sure if that name would stick, and it didn't. He asked his father and me to help him come up with an appropriate name. After all, we did name him initially. After going through about four million choices and some well-meaning friends' choices (oh and a lot of wine), we came up with some ridiculously laughable ideas. Don't worry, the kid laughed too! We even tried some gender-neutral names like Pat or Chris. I tried to coax him into keeping the birth initial so that his initials wouldn't change. Apparently, this whole name concept just added to the dysphoria, so leaving the initial didn't help his cause. Then he came up with Nathan. To be honest, I didn't think it fit his personality, and his father didn't either. But we said to give it go and see if it takes off, and it did.

He went to his counselor and asked if he could have all the teachers call him Nate instead of his birth name (which they call their "death name"—I'm *not* a fan of that term, but I don't really get a say in it) and use the pronoun "he," and the counselor then put it in the school computer system and personally notified all his teachers. I, by the way, am a super fan of this woman! She has asked me to forward any information I find and is hoping to attend the conference in Philly next year. It's not just for my kid. She also sees the influx of LGBTQ+ kids and wants to be prepared for the future. We're just her stepping stone, and I'm glad to help! She's notified the powers that be of his situation, and they're looking into changing his name on all his scholastic files. Nothing will be set in stone until he's changed his gender and name legally, but at least the ball is rolling. The actual files still have his birth name, but any awards, etc., the school uses Nate.

Now like I said, we weren't sure if Nate was going to remain Nate. But I think it's grown on everyone. Here's an interesting sidebar. His father and I were married at the World Trade Center in Manhattan three days before 9/11—quite a memory to have of your wedding. It's not as if we'd want to go back to our wedding venue at this point in our lives, but it's technically no longer there. It's now a museum, irony. I do tend to make light of it by saying it was an omen that our marriage would fail as well. (Sometimes, you need a little levity in these situations.) Anyway, I got pregnant with the kid immediately after, and because of the timing, the location, and the world as it was, we said that if we had a girl, her middle name would be Liberty, and if we had a boy, his middle name would be Justice. Needless to say, we gave birth to a girl. Nate knows all this and has chosen to keep Liberty as an ode to a historical date. I did say that he could change it to Justice as that's what it would've been had he been born a boy, and he said it wasn't necessary. Did I mention that I love this kid? Of course, when he does something stupid, Nathaniel Liberty is my piercing term of endearment. Now that stuck!

Chapter 7

The Process

As we go through this whole process, we've learned quite a lot. One of the most important aspects is the time line. Calling him Nate is important. Calling him "he" is important—all for his mental well-being. The first step, however, is not to legally change the name. That actually comes a little later.

These are the processes we've learned along the way:

1. Accepting your child, friend, coworker, dad, a person of choice for who they are and nothing else.
2. Trying to use the correct pronouns, names, etc. to help them in this process.
3. Buying a whole new damn wardrobe for the said child because, well, duh. (The good news about this point is that I never spent any real money on my clothes but did for the child, so now I have a brand name hand-me-down wardrobe! Luckily, we were similar in size). LOL.
4. Coming out—getting family, friends, school, work, etc. to adhere to this change, use the correct name and pronouns, and simply accept them for who they are becoming.

Then comes the harder parts:

5. Finding a doctor that specializes in transitioning in your area (see chapter 8).
6. Transitioning.
7. Legally changing his name and gender.
8. Beginning a new life.

Chapter 8

What's Up, Doc?

We started at absolute zero! We knew nothing. We knew no one. In a brief conversation one day between Nate's stepmother and a friend, the friend, who happens to be a therapist, mentioned a transgender health expo in Philadelphia. Since Philly isn't far away, we all decided to make a weekend out of it. It's a free event and one of the best experiences and saddest experiences of my life.

Best Experience—I Learned So Much

Nate and I went (my husband couldn't leave work), and we met Nate's dad and stepmom there. I cannot tell you how much we learned! It was a convention—thousands of transgender people from all walks of life, from eight to eighty years old! There were meet and greets, doctor Q&As, college forums, etc. We met and spoke with the most amazing, accepting, loving people. The kid made fun of me for bringing a notebook, but two forums in, he had "borrowed" the notebook and hadn't stopped writing!

Every bathroom was temporarily deemed gender-neutral, except one. There was a specific guarded bathroom for mothers and their small children—understandably so. This was a learning experience for everyone, and some people were definitely not entirely ready. There was a free in-house day care so that parents could attend discussions without the interruption of tired or over-inquisitive young children.

We were curious about the guarded, roped-off bathroom (before I learned of the day care), and we were also lost. I approached the security guard, who was literally staring through me, to ask where I could find a specific discussion room. She never flinched. I asked again. Nothing. After waving my arms around for a few seconds, she finally snapped out of it and looked me in the eye inquisitively. I again asked where I could find room 120. Her response to me was "I have no idea what I just saw." And my response to her was "I think you picked the wrong weekend to work here." At that point, I understood why they had posted her at the children's bathroom, but I was at a loss as to how they didn't explain to her the definition of transgender before appointing her to her post that day. Like I said, some people were not entirely ready.

We found that there were different types of top surgery. If you feel it's necessary (some FTMs do not), there are a few types of augmentation for the FTM, which depend greatly on what they're looking to do. FYI, an FTM is a female-to-male person. An MTF is a male-to-female person.

It is extremely important to have good pectoral muscles beforehand so that the surgeon can decipher where to make the incision to make the scarring less obvious. MTF augmentation is a little more recognizable, as cis-women have been doing it for years. (A cis-woman is a woman who identifies as the gender from which she was born.) The doctors also suggest that you be in the best shape you can before starting the process, as it makes any surgery easier.

Another reason to be in the best shape that you can is that taking hormones completely changes your body. I personally know more about the FTM, but simply speaking, when the MTF starts estrogen, all their body/face/head hair begins to change. The fat around the waist works its way to the hips, chest, and thighs. The body tends to shift a bit, and the sex drive gets knocked down a peg or two. And like puberty, there's mood swings and acne to add to the list. That's the limit of my knowledge on the MTF changes.

My advice would be to attend a seminar or convention to learn as much as you can. I can't possibly stress this enough! The conference in Philadelphia is very enlightening—and free!

I have a little more information on the FTM. It also seems to be a bit more complicated. Once a person starts on testosterone, there are a lot of changes. Like the MTF, the fat shifts. It makes its way to the middle versus the hips, thighs, and chest. Most times, the breast size will shrink, but it varies per individual. They could lose up to a cup size, depending on their initial cup size and fat percentage. That's why it's best to be fit. There's less chance of getting a pudgy middle and increasing the risk of heart disease and diabetes.

Now if an FTM starts off with an A cup, he may not need or want top surgery, as the testosterone could minimize it enough to subdue the dysphoria. Facial hair begins to grow, and the voice starts to deepen after several months. Hair patterns should mimic the maternal grandfather, but that's not a definite response. I was told that the testosterone does not affect the eggs, but extraction and freezing eggs are not uncommon in case you'd like your biological children in the future and don't want to stop taking testosterone in the process of achieving that. They also stop menstruating. And just like puberty, acne could rear its ugly head as well as the mood swings. There is one side effect of testosterone that I didn't see coming, and if you're easily offended, please skip to the next paragraph. The size of the clitoris changes. It grows, and as I've never seen this process, I am told that it could grow as much as an inch or so, which would make it what is termed a "micropenis." And again, if the FTM is okay with that, there could be no desire or need for bottom surgery. Quite the information, no?

If an FTM stops taking testosterone, they will begin menstruating again, and the fat will shift back. The hair and voice changes will most likely not revert to their original state. And if top surgery was performed, they will not regain breasts—maybe a little shifted fat but no more than that. They can, however, at this point, possibly get pregnant.

FTM bottom surgery, from what I hear, is extremely complicated and not 100 percent effective, as it could very well be rejected by the body. Luckily, at this point in my son's transition, he does not feel he will need bottom surgery and hoping for a little more than an Angry Inch.

MTF bottom surgery is not as complicated, but it's definitely not a simple operation and definitely not reversible from what I've been told.

We left with names of doctors (good and bad), information from twenty other FTMs on which direction to head first, what to ask a college before applying, and a million other important pieces of the puzzle.

Of course, this is just loosely what I learned at the expo, and I don't even remotely say that I'm an expert, and I advise finding an expo to make sure you're getting all the information you need. This book is just a beginning to give you a little insight so that you aren't starting at zero!

Saddest Experience at the Expo—I Learned Too Much

Pride Day had recently passed before attending the expo, and I had bought myself a T-shirt that says, "Free Bear Mom Hugs," with a transgender flag logo in the background. I decided to bring it and wear it at the expo. This was probably the best decision I had made that day, outside of attending in general.

When I said earlier that there were about two thousand transgender people at the conference, that was a fair assumption, but I could not give you the actual number. They were mostly teenagers and twenty-somethings, with some ranging to their forties. Some were even older, and a few were on the younger than the teen side. The much younger ones were there with their parents. Outside of those few, I'd say there were about ten or so accepting sets of parents looking to be informed. We were told upon entry to avoid eye or physical contact with anyone outside the facility that was protesting, and there were guards posted at all entrances to make sure only love walked in those doors. This, my friends, is the saddest thing I've ever seen.

I'd say that the majority of attendees were alone teens, with no parents to help or love or accept them. I'm tearing up now just thinking about what I saw. These children were unaccepted at home—some even thrown out of their homes. There were runaways. The ones I spoke to "and hugged" had found their niche, found help, found love. But the one thing they all said to me was that they'd wished their parents had done what I did. They wished that they'd chosen to be informed, not be ignorant of something no one can control.

There was one young man that I will *never forget*! His name, on the other hand, I can't remember. He was in the top surgery meet and greet. He is a gorgeous young man and had had the most amazing surgery that was almost impossible to even tell that he had. His nipples had remained intact because he was not very well endowed as a woman. So we approached him to ask questions about his doctors and surgeons. The who, where, when, and how much questions were really the top of our list. Upon approaching, the first comment I had for each of them was if they felt uncomfortable speaking with a cis-woman as well as my transgender child, I would happily step back. Not one young man felt that need, as they were delighted to inform me as well—which made me very happy.

After speaking formally on medical topics with this one young man for a few minutes, I shamelessly told him how handsome he was. That's when I noticed the tears in his eyes. I immediately dropped everything and asked him if he needed a hug. Boy, did he ever! It turned into a group hug. Once we were all in tears, I asked him what was wrong. He told me his story. At about the age of seventeen, he came out to his parents as transgender. His parents were not accepting. They tried to "fix" him, and when that failed, they threw him out. Thankfully, he had a very accepting and loving girlfriend at the time who left with him. They found work and school, and he found doctors and hormones as best he could. He said that he got lucky with a good ending to the surgery, but the surgeon he had was cold and had no bedside manner, and in addition, he had wound up with an infection from the surgery and found himself back in the hospital, at which time the surgeon had washed her hands of him and moved on. Soon after, so did the girlfriend. He did all this alone—young, so very young, and alone.

He since turned out just fine. He has a good job and a new girlfriend and is happy and healthy—both mentally and physically. But he was still saddened by what his family let him go through alone because they just didn't understand. So he thanked me. "For what?" I asked. He thanked me for being there for my son, for asking questions, for trying to wipe away ignorance, for the hugs.

During the rest of our time there, I couldn't help but look at all the people there alone and hope that they have a happy ending as well and that they're not tormented emotionally by a family that couldn't accept "different." I ran into that young man on several occasions during the next couple of days at the expo, and each time, he got a big hug, a really big hug, and so did a lot of others!

Sure it ended on a happy note for him, for us, but that has to have been one of the saddest experiences of my life—to know that people just gave up on what should be unconditional love.

Still a Great Experience

We learned a lot that weekend—more than we knew was even available. I know I sound like a broken record, but do your research, experience as much as you can, as soon as you can. My little blurb here is only the beginning.

A reminder though, the medical process, the mental therapy. Find a good therapist who specializes in dysphoria.

Find a doctor and surgeon that fit *you*! Don't feel obligated. If you or your kid don't mesh, don't use them. You may lose a consultation fee, but it'll be worth it in the end. There are plenty of doctors these days. If they're not in your area, take a road trip. If you want to find more information on doctors, find an expo in your area, or find a mom or trans-friendly private group on social media. Do your research. Don't accept someone you can't smile with.

The first physical step is hormone therapy. Whether it's estrogen or testosterone, make sure you're in a good physical and mental state before beginning what will be the start of a beautiful new life!

Then you can have the necessary surgeries for your well-being. Take your time though. Do all your research. I can't state this enough. We saw so many surgeries gone wrong because people were in a hurry. You have your whole life ahead of you. Take your time, and do it right!

And last but not least, legally change your gender and name. None of this is free. There is financial help available through our government. A good doctor or lawyer can help. There are pro bono lawyers available, but they're not everywhere and not for everyone.

Once you or your loved one have made it this far, this is it! This is the beginning of a beautiful life. It's not to say that it will be easy from this point forward. It won't be, and there will still be times when they can't just say I'm a guy/girl. They'll have to say I'm a transgender guy/girl. And that's okay! Remember that. It'll be necessary for medical treatment, and I'd advise it when dating. You'll want to make sure any insurance you have covers hormone therapy as well because you'll be on hormones for the rest of your life—at least most of it. So if they don't, there are places available that will help. I know there's one in Manhattan and one in Los Angeles. I'm sure there are more, and I expect you'll find them in larger cities.

Chapter 9

Coming Out

Okay, so I knew he was transgender. Well, all four parents knew, and we'd told all four families. They accepted it. They've begun using the correct pronoun (for the most part), and they called him Nate. He was even invited to an all-male golf outing in my husband's family! Now I am sure that there is a lot of talk behind our backs. Is that okay? No, not really. But am I ignorant enough to believe it isn't happening? No, not at all.

I get it. It's not a common way of life. Not yet, anyway. Just thirty years ago, people were shunned for being gay. Just sixty years ago, black people weren't allowed to sit at the counter with whites. And not long before that, women couldn't wear pants or vote. Bob Dylan said, "The times they are a-changin'," and people need to change with them. It just takes some people longer than others. As my mother would say, "Get over it." And this time, she's right. Sooner or later, you need to get over it 'cause it's not going away, not today, not tomorrow, not ever. Women, nonwhites, gays, transgenders, we're all here to stay, so get over it.

So after the family was aware and informed, I decided to take my journey to social media. Just before school started, I publicly posted the following online:

Dear friends and family,

With the new school year approaching, I decided that it was time to make a PSA. It's a brave new world out there, and in this time of turmoil, I ask you all to be more open-minded and stop the hate!

Let's call this my gender reveal announcement! "The kid" will be legally changing his name this year to Nate/Nathan, Nathaniel (when I'm mad 😆). He uses pronouns he/him. Physical changes will also be occurring this year as he begins his physical transition.

I have always been a supporter of the LGBTQ+ community and will always support my child as he makes his way through life!

This change will not be easy, and I ask that if you are unable to support him as well, please hide my page or unfriend me on social media, as we do not need the unnecessary hate. I'm content to breeze past any anti-transgender posts on your page without comment. Please return the favor! I will also unfriend anyone who spews hate. We understand that using the correct pronoun is not easy yet, but in time, it does get easier and will be even easier once he starts to look more "male." I still screw up on occasion!

This has not been easy on him, but he has a huge support team that loves him dearly, including four loving parents!

So I ask you, if you see him on the street, in school, on social media, just give a wave and say, "Hey, Nate." You'd be surprised how easy it is to be nice and make someone happy!

Renee

And *poof*, our family journey went public. It was not easy to do, and I expected backlash from the ignorant. However much I was expecting people to unfriend me, block me, ignore me, that's not what I received. We received an outpouring of love and support from everyone—and I mean everyone! In addition to the liberal moms I knew would be there for us, staunch republicans came out in support of Nate! The multitude of "deplorable" friends we have apparently are not as hateful as the media is making people think. That's it on politics—I just wanted it known that we've got really good friends!

The funny part was the friends that IM'd me or texted to tell me that if I needed to talk, they were there for me. I got such a kick out of this. Why? Because we'd been going through this for three years. I was good! I didn't need to "talk" to anyone. I wasn't upset or scared. I'd been through it, and it was just time to go public. What I did realize, however, was that *they* needed to talk! They had questions. They were curious. They didn't want to be ignorant either!

So I had some dinners with friends and some online conversations. Some friends came over and talked over a bottle of wine. But it wasn't for my kid or me. It was for them, for their understanding! And *that* was what I appreciated, even though they had no idea that's what they were doing! Like I said, "Funny!" And that's why I felt the need to write this all down—for them and for the ones who didn't reach out but are still curious, for the social media stalkers who read every word and never say but one, and for the moms who have no idea where to start! Sure, this isn't for everyone, but what is?

Does that mean that people aren't still talking behind our backs? Again, no. I had an issue with someone I had previously unfriended (for other reasons). We have a great deal of mutual friends. Some of which remain friends with him only to feed me his relentless online tales of my imaginary life. I found it humorous, for the most part, seriously though, what was I to do. Anyone who knows me, knows they are lies, so let him dig his own hole. Until he said something about my kid, and I received the screenshot. My husband had him take it down, which was fine, a little late, but fine. And to be honest, I wasn't particularly shocked that he had something to say about the subject—annoyed yes, but shocked, not so much. What hurt me and dug deep into my soul was that he had somehow found out about it. My account is private. This meant that one of those mutual friends is a backstabber. That hurts! Yes, people talk behind our backs. We've established that. However, every one of our friends knows that this man hates me, hates my kid, and yet they still found the time to talk about us to *him*. This disgusts me! And those are the people that worry me.

If they're willing to support my kid in public or ask questions about our situation, that's at least a step in the right direction. Maybe try not to talk about us to haters, that may be a bit more helpful. Maybe they're using my conversations with them as fodder for a conversation with someone else. Maybe. But at least now they have the correct information. I'd rather people used my words to talk about me than make something up that they are completely ignorant about and most likely false statements. Maybe it's not a giant leap for mankind, but it's something, right?

Chapter 10

We Have a Wee Problem

Prior to his social media coming out party, I'd gone to the high school with a request. This was during the summer between sophomore and junior year. Previously, the transgender kids that were uncomfortable in their gender-assigned bathroom were given the choice of using the nurse's bathroom in addition to their assigned gender's bathroom. This worked well for a while. Literally, it worked when there were only three or four transgender kids in the school.

Now I know that this amount of kids may be more normal in our area of the country than it is outside of a metropolitan area. But it may not. This is truly not limited to our area. I'm just afraid that what causes this limitation is only fear. There are most likely as many kids in rural Indiana as there are in our suburb of New York City. But because of nonacceptance and fear, they don't come out. This adds to the percentage rates of teen suicide, transgender and gay teen suicide especially.

So because I'm involved in the kid's life in a big way, I knew that the influx of freshmen this year had quite a number of transgender kids that were going to make the nurse's daily activities that much more difficult. In addition, Nathan was going to start physically transitioning this year. So how do you send your kid to gym class when he's always used the girls' locker room and he certainly doesn't look like a boy anymore?

Freshman year, there was an incident in the locker room. Nothing horrible, just some snotty girls who, spewing among themselves, I mean speaking, chose to ask each other why "that kid" had to change down to skin during gym. And "Ew, those are hairy armpits" didn't help either. The kid came home in tears. So Mama Bear went to school. I met with the gym teacher, who had no idea that this was happening. She promised me that this would never happen again, and she would stand watch while the kid changed for gym. He was also given the choice of using the girls' bathroom right outside the gym, which really didn't make a bit of difference, but at least they made an effort. (Now for those I've lost, he wears a binder to hide his chest.) You cannot exercise and therefore take gym in a binder without causing damage. Therefore, he changed out of the binder and into a sports bra for gym. (This apparently caused trauma for the average VSCO girl.) The teacher watching the area was fine and worked well temporarily.

So here we are. Once he starts testosterone, he will start looking more and more masculine. This will not fly in the girls' locker room. On the other hand, he still has the parts that are not acceptable in the boys' locker room either.

Hence my requests—there were two. Luckily, I graduated from the same high school that Nate is attending, and I had a pretty good lay of the land, albeit a hundred years ago. I played sports and used the girls' team room. This team room is no longer used by the teams as they use the locker rooms in the gym so that they're only taking up space in one locker. There is also a boys' team room, but it is connected to the boys' locker room and a walk-through for the boys—so that wouldn't work. So request #1, let the transgender kids use the girls' team room regardless of FTM or MTF. That room has lockers and showers and toilets and individually curtained-off changing areas. You'd have thought this was a no-brainer! It was seemingly best for everyone. The cis-girls wouldn't be uncomfortable, the cis-boys wouldn't be uncomfortable, and the transgender kids would have a place in which they could feel comfortable. Request #2, again, as I knew the high school footprint and several employees of the school, I knew that there were two locked, unused bathrooms on premises.

All they have to do is open one to a gender-neutral population. Some surrounding towns have gender-neutral bathrooms already in place. I obtained pictures and videos and sent them to the school so they could evaluate their situation and come to some sort of similar compliance. Again, make everyone happy. No-brainer, right? Yeah, not so much.

I met with a school administrator, and he liked all my suggestions and assured me that the two requests would be handled before school began. A few days before school, he called me to bring the kid and come in. We saw the team room all cleaned and ready for the transgender kids to use on an as-needed basis, which I think was helped along by my friend in the custodial department. You could clearly see the happiness on the kid's face! Step one done! And it continues to work perfectly!

The admin once again assured me that the bathroom situation would be handled before school started as well. I told him about an unused bathroom I knew of in the art hall (which is a very convenient location for some very artsy teens). He said he'd check into it. School started—no bathroom. I continued to annoy him, especially since we had the flu and coxsackie outbreak (yes, among teens, go figure), and the healthy transgender kids had to use the same bathroom as the contagious kids. This was taking way too long. Finally, after my vague threat of going to the board of education and the local news, we got our gender-neutral bathroom. I don't think they meant to drag their feet. It just wasn't their first priority, whereas my kid's mental state is mine.

It's locked at all times, and there's "usually" a security guard in that corridor that's supposed to let them in. Apparently, they're afraid of bullying and misuse, hence it being locked. I'll give them that one. The guard is not always available, but more times than not, someone is there. Nate has made friends with the custodial and security staff (as I said, they all love him), and there's usually someone nearby to let him in. He's advised the other transgender kids to do the same. Again, this isn't perfect, but it's a step in the right direction.

I tell you all this because these steps can all be done. It takes time, it takes lots of patience, and it certainly takes some moxie and making enemies. Well, maybe not enemies, but I'm sure there's a bunch of people calling me a pain in the ass. Once again, maybe they don't say it to my face, but let me remind you, I'm the size of a running back, and I really don't give a shit what people think of me outside of my little circle. So avoiding me is probably smart on their part. And, like I said before, a funny thing happened to this bear mom on the way to fifty.

Do I wish it was standard practice that all public bathrooms were single-unit gender-neutral facilities? Sure! In a new building, yes. But I understand not getting it in a hundred-year-old school. Baby steps! We do have a new local Barnes and Noble that has six separate single-stall bathrooms. And my little troop of geeks and misfits are in heaven!

Chapter 11

Parents

In my life and research, I've come across a few types of parents of transgender kids.

First, there's the unconditionally loving and accepting, helpful parents—four of which I believe Nate has. Sometimes, this parent pushes a little too hard at the first sign of a difference. We all want our kids to stand out in some way. I would not have chosen this way, but it certainly wasn't a choice of mine or Nate's. It wasn't a choice at all. Sometimes, we need to back off a little and let life take care of itself.

There was recently a court case in the news regarding a mother of young twin boys who were transitioning one into a girl. The parents were divorced, and the father was not on board simply because, during the time that he spent with the twins, he never saw any signs. So they went to court. The court findings sided with the father after speaking in chambers with the twins, watching videos, etc. According to the court, the mother realized she wasn't going to have another child and decided that she wanted one of each. These are the scary people—the ones with an agenda that only hurt their children more and provide society with anti-transgender fodder. Now could the father honestly have the agenda not to have a transgender child? Possibly, and it's possible that will be brought up in some sort of appeal. But the judge saw no signs in his chamber, and neither did the twin brother, so I'm siding with the courts on this one.

Next, you have the somewhat accepting parent that refuses to acknowledge the legitimacy of the life their child is not currently enjoying. They love their child and accept that they're different but refuse to help in any way, whether they think it's a phase or just a scream for attention. Occasionally, they might be right, but they're not necessarily helpful. These are the parents that need the most help. They're not willing to look for it themselves and may not show their kid enough attention on the subject. If you're that parent, I hope you've thought this through, and I want you to go hug your kid right now. Go!

Then you have the parents that just plain refuse to believe that their kid is anything other than what's considered normal. We have kids because we want kids (usually), but they're going to lose these kids over time. They believe it's tough love when they throw them out of the house for not conforming. Somewhere in their warped minds, they think they're doing the right thing. These are the parents that brought tears to my eyes at the convention. They weren't there, of course not, but their children were alone and scared—still gay and transgender. Their tough love didn't change that and won't, and I can't comprehend how they thought it would. To those parents, lose the ego, drop the hate, go find your kid, show them home. Home isn't necessarily your house. It's in your heart! Go right now, go, before it's too late!

On that note, I want to go back to talking about the conference. There was a little kid there, maybe eight, with his mother. I am going to be completely honest here. I was a little worried. I bring you back to that recent court case that I mentioned earlier in this chapter.

My immediate opinion was that there was another mother pushing an overbearing agenda on this child and, therefore, just assuming the opposite of what most of us do. We, the average cis-parent, assume our child is society's "normal," a straight, heterosexual, cisgender human until proven otherwise. We want to believe that our child is unique, special, one of a kind. Whereas, there is a small percentage that assumes their child is just as unique, special, one of a kind, but also in the 1 percent that is transgender just because they showed some possible signs at an early age. These parents not only accept their child for who they are but also they almost drive these children further in that direction—sometimes very rightfully so. But other times, they may be pushing a desire for something special past where it rightfully belongs. Without that push, would a child simply be gay, if even part of the LGBTQ+ community at all? But with that parental push, would s/he no longer sees themself correctly and dysphoria ensues? I have no idea which it was in this instance. Hopefully, this was a transgender child with euphoria and a very accepting mom and nothing more.

I do know, however, that the young person was in a Q&A session with a doctor and asked all the right questions. They asked important medical questions necessary for a young transgender human. Were they Mommy's questions that they rightfully memorized? Or were they legitimate questions that a young transgender person would want to know? I'll never know. There are two ways that this child is going to go—either exactly where they need to go with a very supportive home or way down a rabbit hole that wasn't meant to be because of an agenda.

I think about this child all the time as well. I still worry about them because I don't know the child or the mother. But I hope that every question s/he asked was his/her own and not something forced upon him. My opinion leans toward the questions being his/her own, and my fingers are crossed because sometimes that just what you have to do.

They did ask about puberty blockers. Now I'm going to assume that the young child was born male because they were worried about puberty blockers causing them to continue to grow for too long, and they would then be very tall. I don't recall the answer, but I do remember that blockers do affect the growth hormones. I'm afraid I got lost in thought and didn't listen further as it didn't affect Nate since he's in and/or past puberty.

Testosterone will also affect height if the growth plates are not closed. In other words, if a teen FTM starts testosterone and his growth plates have not yet closed, he can still have a growth spurt. This is why a lot of FTMs want to start testosterone as early as possible to avoid being a shorter man. There is a test to see if the plates have closed. There are no specific side effects that they know of for this type of hormone therapy at an early age; however, we really don't have the forty-year data that most long-term testing allows us. There wasn't a large population of transgender people forty years ago to take into consideration as to how it has affected them. This scared me. The last thing I want is to do something that I assume will make my child happy, only to find out that we caused cancer twenty years down the road. On the other hand, if we don't follow this road, I may very well have a suicidal child. It's a very slippery slope, and we need to tread carefully. We chose to continue to stick close to a good therapy schedule, laugh as often as possible, and wait 'til he was seventeen before starting hormone therapy. I have no idea if this was the right decision, but it was ours.

Chapter 12

Sexuality versus Gender

Right now, someone is reading that last chapter and saying that age eight is too young to know. This is where I've had countless conversations with people just trying to understand what's going on here.

I don't know how many times I've seen on TV or heard in a conversation online or in person that we shouldn't be discussing sexuality with an eight-year-old; therefore, an eight-year-old cannot know if they are transgender or not. Right or wrong, that's a bird of a different color.

Here's the misnomer. Being transgender has absolutely nothing to do with sexuality. It is not about who or what you are attracted *to*! Being transgender is a mental state of how you see *yourself*! If you don't see yourself in the body that's developing, you don't understand why you have to wear certain things, cut your hair a certain way, play with certain toys, or even go into certain types of work (sadly), you may be transgender. Or you may not. But this has absolutely nothing to do with who you are attracted to, or by means, sexuality.

You can be transgender and still be gay or straight or bi or so many, many other options that I've recently learned of. For instance, my son is a transgender boy. He is still attracted to men, mostly. I'm pretty sure he feels that love is love, regardless of the individual he finds attractive, and I'm sure given a chance, he'd go in whatever direction pointing to love. However, he does find himself attracted mostly to males, be they transgender, bi, or just straight-up gay. He calls himself a gay boy. This confuses a lot of people, especially in my generation. I think a majority of the younger generation may have figured it all out for the most part, but we take a little more time.

What I'm trying to say is that just because someone sees themself as a man instead of a woman does not mean that they're also attracted to women just because they see themself as a man. Okay, I realize that still may not make sense to some. But read it a few times and let it sink in.

Now with that, there are certain people in the LGBTQ+ community that want to take the *T* out of it for just that reason. Transgender is just that—gender, not sexuality. Since the LGBQ all stand for sexualities, why should there be a letter that stands for gender? This then adds to the confusion for a tremendous amount of cis-people.

Well, here's my take, my opinion if you will. I'm not a doctor and don't profess to be the most knowledgeable person on the subject, but it just seems like common sense to me. Let's say you take the *T* out, where are transgender people going to go? Are we not all allies? If you take the *T* out, they're once again outcast and alone. So to anyone in that small percentage reading this, let it be. Let them be! They need allies just as much, if not more than the rest of the community! And hell, some of them fit into the other letters as well as the *T*, like my son.

Chapter 13

Safe House

You can't spell community without *unity*. We live in a town that prides itself on its stigma-free unison. We don't have a huge LGBTQ+ community, but we have a gloriously supportive community! We have a town-wide stigma-free program. The high school has a pride club, the teachers are supportive, and most parents are watching the LGBTQ kids' backs. I happen to be friends with a custodian at the school (yes, small town), and he'll text me if he sees Nate looking sad. There are teachers looking out for him. Did I mention the fantastic counselor? Nate will even occasionally have cookies and chat with the principal. The mayor (the Republican mayor) will seek him out and make sure he's doing all right if he happens to see him at a function.

However, not *all* the parents are supportive. There are some of the "refuse to accept" parents and some of the "ignore it, it'll go away" parents. Sadly, these parents are not going anywhere anytime soon either. What the kids do know is that my house is open, supportive parent or not. If they're being bothered, if they just need to study somewhere peaceful and have a cup of coffee or tea, as long as my kid is there, they're welcome too. I don't necessarily trust some of the other parents; hence my kid has to be there as well. Once they're eighteen and they want to come over and have tea and chew my ear off or just have a nonjudgmental place to crash for a few hours, they're more than welcome. That, they know as well. And that's true for any kid, not just the LGBTQs. But this little band of misfits holds the key to my heart (sans the little trending alpha bully until that one changes their tune), especially the ones who can't talk to their own parents.

There's another set of parents. These are the ones I try to keep my distance from because I won't lie to another parent. I may not be particularly forthcoming if I don't think they're accepting, but I won't lie. These are also the parents that I can't particularly invite into my house—not because I don't like them but because I still have Nate's baby pictures up around the house, and there's a lot of pink. And while these parents may or may not be accepting, they don't always know that Nate is transgender and have only known him as a boy. They all adore him and welcome him into their homes, but now would they if they knew? If their own children aren't telling them, then that tells me something.

Then there are the parents that I've known for a few years whose children are gay or bi or "?" and still don't even know that's the case in their own home. They also have no idea why their children are calling my "daughter" Nate. Again, if their kids aren't talking, I'm certainly not going to "out" them. So they come over, and I see the kid cringe when they use his "dead" name. But I've told him that it's up to him to set them straight. I'm not driving this bus, and Nate's old enough to drive it himself. I'm sorry that I'm not perfect, but I am still learning…every day! And I'm still changing and adapting…every day.

Should I take down the baby pictures? Probably. But I can't yet get myself to do it. It's a process for all of us. At some point, I will, maybe. Maybe I'll just tell anyone who asks that I had a daughter, which is not a lie. I don't know what direction I'll head yet. All I know for sure is that I had a great daughter, and now I have a great son. No more, no less.

Chapter 14

Making Friends

Nate has no problem making friends. All the adults love him, and so do most of the kids. Do they think he's a little weird? Probably, but that doesn't take away from the fact that they honestly like him. He's smart, talented, fun, and goofy. He's a protector of the kids in his group that don't speak up for themselves. What's not to love?

Me, the bear mom, I'm a little different. I'm also protective, but I'm a strong-willed, take no shit, pain in the ass as well. I consider myself pretty smart, especially street-smart, yet I'm forgetful and can certainly do stupid crap. I stayed in the same town that I grew up in right outside of Manhattan. My husband is from that same small town. We know almost everyone, and just about everyone is a cisgender mom or dad—which means I don't know a lot of people in the gay community. (The few I do know are fabulous, however!)

So where do I begin to find someone in my shoes? Being a small town where everyone knows someone, I was introduced to some gay moms who, in turn, knew someone who is transgender. I also found a mom whose son came out as transgender quietly a few years back. We became online friends—the mom and the son! Now when that mom said, "If you ever need to talk," I thought, *Yeah, I could probably talk to her.* Not because I needed to talk to someone, but because I needed an ally as well as someone with some inside knowledge. The son was able to give me more information. He linked us to better binders, steps to take, etc. He introduced us to some doctors and opened some doors that we hadn't even seen when we looked at the wall.

Did I just get lucky? Once again, maybe. But all this information is available. There are social media pages just for us. There are conferences and classes and podcasts. The information is out there to learn as much as we can! You just have to look for it or be that friendly neighborhood pushy pain in the ass.

Chapter 15

A New Beginning

So here I sit, writing about our experiences. It's been quite the journey, and we're only maybe halfway there, at most. I started off as one of those people who would giggle at the Caitlyn Jenner memes. Now I cringe—although I give her some serious credit. I recently saw her on a celebrity roast. It wasn't her roast, but boy did those comedians roast her—easy target, I guess. But she took it all in stride and laughed heartily at her own expense. I gained an extraordinary amount of respect for her that day! I'm welling up just thinking about it. She has got to be the mentally strongest person on this planet! To come out at her age, the public transition, the humility, the humanity—I can't fathom what that woman's gone through! And, damn, she's got great legs!

And speaking of Caitlyn Jenner, I believe she's still attracted to women. This drives home the point that gender and sexuality are not the same. She's now a lesbian or bisexual but also transgender because one has nothing to do with the other, as you can see.

I don't think I was ever a bad person. I do think I've always been a pretty good mom. Did I buy a leash after the kid ran off in Kohl's and I had a search party on him? Yup! Did I scream at him at a swim party when he was being an asshole and I made the other moms jump? Yup! Did my husband move me to the porch when the kid was three 'cause I may or may not have wanted to beat the crap out of him for dropping an Ikea bookshelf on me (quite an accomplishment, I may add)? Yup! (And no, I didn't beat him, don't worry.) But I did what I had to do.

And I still do. We're moms. We're dads. We do the best that we can for our children. And after seventeen years, this kid has made me a better person. He's made me want to be a better person. And because of him, I think I am! I even had a teacher tell me that Nate makes him a better teacher! Crap, my eyes are welling up again, makes it hard to type.

I get the occasional "You're such a great mom" from someone because I'm supportive. Aren't we all supposed to be supportive of our kids? I'm not a great mom. I'm just a mom doing mom things for a kid who's not just a kid but a great kid doing kid things—not average kid things. That's for sure!

If this book enlightens or comforts just one parent, friend, coworker, or just plain makes them a little bit of a better person, then I've accomplished what I set out to do. If you meet a transgender person, be kind, say hi. It's that easy. You don't have to become their best friend. They just want to be accepted as humans because that's all they are…human.

On to phase 2 of this journey—the transition—we'll see how this goes. One baby step at a time. I'll keep a log and write again. I can't wait to see how this turns out! I hope I got you interested too!

I look forward to a world of happy androgynous mocha people. I'm probably not going to see it. But I have a dream.

About the Author

Renee Masterson-Carr has always had a passion for writing, whether it be poetry, lyrics, or storytelling. Her poetry was first published when she was a teen. Now with a teen of her own, Renee has years of stories to share.

Adopted by her stepfather at a young age, she went from a "mom and me" home to an instantly large family with three new siblings and lots of extended families. That, along with a diversified background of bookkeeping, office management, and construction, has given her the capacity to deal with just about anything life throws at her. The somewhat unexpected dissolution of the marriage to her son's father greatly enhanced the ability to adapt to life's little obstacles.

In a small town just outside of New York City, Renee purchased her childhood home and raised her family in that house. Like "Norm from Cheers," everybody in town knows her name. A construction worker by day, she's known to her family and friends as dependable and fierce, with a soft side for the people she loves.

She shares her home with her son and supportive husband (from the same small town) as well as her retired parents. Renee has always tried to donate time to causes that are close to her heart—usually involving seniors' or children's needs and, of course, dogs. She enjoys taking "weird adventures" around the country with her husband and son and sometimes a spare friend for the road because if life's not about anything else, it's about the journey.

CPSIA information can be obtained
at www.ICGtesting.com
Printed in the USA
LVHW092229031120
670651LV00008B/379

9 781662 413933